Needlepoint Designs
for Beginners

Books by William Halsey Brister:

THE NEEDLEPOINT CAT

NEEDLEPOINT DESIGNS FOR BEGINNERS

Needlepoint Designs
for Beginners

30 EXCITING PROJECTS
TO DECORATE EVERY ROOM
OF YOUR HOME

William Halsey Brister

Doubleday & Company, Inc.
Garden City, New York
1986

ACKNOWLEDGMENTS

Special thanks to:

Dennis Barna, of New York City, for all the beautiful color and black-and-white photography.

Jan and Steve Bertwell, of Richmond, Rhode Island, whose business, Finishing Touches, did just that for all the projects in the book.

Nancy Dow who typed the manuscript and had to contend with my spelling and handwriting inadequacies.

LIBRARY OF CONGRESS CATALOGING IN PUBLICATION DATA
Brister, William Halsey, 1934–
Needlepoint designs for beginners.
1. Canvas embroidery—Patterns. I. Title.
TT778.C3B76 1986   746.44′2041   85-10327
ISBN: 0-385-19655-5

This book is dedicated to the late Ray Nash of Dartmouth College whose courses, Bookbinding I & II, and "Let's Make a Valentine," whetted my appetite for the graphic arts.

Contents

Contents

Introduction

Back in 1964, when I first learned to needlepoint, there were very few books on the subject. Most of them were geared to people who already knew the basics and could tackle any of the designs in the books. In the early seventies, needlepoint became big business and it seemed every week a new book on the subject hit the bookstores. Now that the big boom has come and gone, there is once again a dearth of material. I'm sure the people who got hooked on needlepoint have gone on to do their own designs, since what is currently available in kits is limited.

Cross stitch has the limelight today. So when I showed my editor several canvases for new books, she seemed hesitant. She suggested instead a book of designs just for beginners. Thinking back to the time when I started needlepointing, I wished I had had such a book. So that is the reason for this book.

At the height of the renaissance of needlepoint, there were books written drawing on a wide variety of themes from American Indian to American Revolution design. Only a few were really for the novice. I looked at the beginners' books which were done by some talented people, but I found them lacking. The designs were pretty, but extremely simple. I'm not saying simple is bad, but a whole book of unchallenging designs can become boring. So, in this book, we start with the simple, then add a little more outlining or shading as we go along from design to design. By the end of the book, you should be able to master any design and perhaps even create a design of your own.

This past summer I entered a local arts and crafts show. I was amazed at the number of people who came up to me and said how they would love to learn needlepoint, but that it looked too complicated and difficult. I kept telling them it was the easiest thing in the world. Of course, until you try it, you'll never know. Like playing the piano, anybody can learn. The longer you practice, the easier it becomes.

Needlepoint, to me, is only blocks or areas of color which are sometimes connected by outlining. Just think back to the coloring books your parents bought you for a rainy day at home. The only difference is that in needlepoint you cover the black lines. Sometimes you use outlining, but it is not always necessary, as you will see from some of the designs in this book.

Needlepointing is fun and rewarding. You can look at your finished project and say, "Hey, I did that!" You'll not only have an object of art (and needlepoint is an art), but you'll have something that will last more than a lifetime.

Part I
Learning the Basics

Getting Started: The Materials

In my first book, I stated that the only things you need to get started in needlepoint are canvas, yarn, a needle, and a good pair of sharp scissors. To that list I'm adding one more thing—a lot of patience. Developing your skills as a needle-pointer takes time, so don't become frustrated with your first few attempts at projects.

CANVAS

Just as in oil painting, the surface you work on in needlepoint is called canvas. There are three types of canvas: penelope, mono, and mono-interlocking.

The designs in this book have been worked only on the mono-interlocking canvas, and this is what I suggest you use. Penelope canvas has double threads (and takes a different stitch than the one I have used); mono has a single thread which will move up or down, or left and right. If you are a hard puller of stitches, as I am, this moving can cause the next rows of holes to close up, which is annoying. In the mono-interlocking canvas, the single thread is just that—interlocked or stationary—and does not move.

All canvases come in different mesh sizes. In this book, I have used only 10, 12, and 14 mesh size canvas. This simply means that 10 mesh canvas will have ten stitches or holes to the inch, 12 mesh canvas will have twelve stitches or holes to the inch, and so on. The correct mesh size for each design is given at the beginning of the project. When I say correct mesh size, I simply mean the one I have used. The designs can be done on a different mesh size, but if you follow the given graph and are counting the stitches, you will come out with something bigger or smaller than what I have done.

Most shops hate to cut canvas to a specific size, so it is wise to buy a yard or so at a time. You'll have a supply of canvas for future projects. Out of a yard of canvas, you can get four or more large projects.

Most canvas is made of cotton or a blend.

Do not buy or use plastic canvas for any of the designs. Plastic dries up, becomes brittle and breaks. There go all your stitches. The only merit in plastic canvas is that the finished project will not have to be blocked. This is simply not worth the price of a ruined canvas plus your wasted effort. Stay away from plastic canvas.

The last thing I should mention about canvas is the price, which can vary quite a bit from shop to shop. There is no advantage to buying expensive canvas. Just because it was imported from France or Belgium doesn't make it better than an American brand. Most imported canvas, as far as I know, does not come in interlocking weave. The Europeans may have it by now, but it is sure to be expensive. If you can shop around, do so. A yarn outlet or yarn discount store carries all mesh sizes and inexpensive canvas.

YARN

The yarn used in needlepoint is called tapestry, crewel, or Persian yarn. The most often used yarn is the Persian (100 percent wool) or Persian type (acrylic). Persian yarn consists of three strands, and each strand is made up of two plies. A strand is merely the unit, while a ply is part of a strand.

For all the canvas sizes in this book, you use only *two* strands. Cut a length of yarn (no more than 18 inches); pull one strand off. Use this to measure the next length of yarn. Pull one strand off your second length and match the other single strand. You will now have three sets of yarn ready to use.

Yarn is sold either by weight (ounces) or by length (yards in skeins). An ounce is about 40 yards. A skein will have somewhere from 8 to 12 yards. For each design, I have given the approximate yards of yarn you will need to finish the project. Determining the amount of yarn to use is difficult (unless you have kept a written account), since everybody works differently. I have a tendency to pull tightly, and this uses less yarn. A person with a light touch, or a beginner, will use more yarn. The beginner will make mistakes and will have to rip out the stitches. The yarn from a pulled-out section should not be used again. A good rule of thumb for the amount of yarn to use when you are doing your own designs is as follows: to cover 1 square inch of 10 mesh canvas, you need 1¼ yards of two-strand yarn; to cover 1 square inch of 12 mesh canvas, 1½ yards of two-strand yarn; to cover 1 square inch of 14 mesh canvas, you need 1¾ yards of two-strand yarn.

Once again, most of you know that wool is expensive, so I say shop around. Some well-known manufacturers of Persian yarn are Bucilla, Columbia-Minerva, DMC and Paternayan. With all these companies producing yarn, the color range is amazing for any shade or hue. The shade of color can and does vary from dye lot to dye lot, so I suggest you overbuy at a single time. There is nothing more frustrating than running out of a color and trying to match it without a dye lot number. The leftover yarn can be used for other projects. I have bags of it.

I found a marvelous Persian-type yarn called Red Heart made by Coats and Clark and available in most dime stores. You can write to their Consumer Service Department, P.O. Box 1966, Stamford, Connecticut 06904, for a color chart and order forms. It is made of 100 percent Creslan, an acrylic fiber. I recommend it for several good reasons: it is inexpensive, it doesn't fuzz up or fray as wool tends to do, and it glides or pulls through the threads of the canvas easily and smoothly, whereas sometimes with pure wool it seems like a tug-of-war.

NEEDLES

The needle used in needlepoint is called a tapestry needle, made of steel, with a large eye for easy threading, and a blunt end. When I first saw the needle, I thought how clever to have a blunt point —no punctured and bandaged fingers. However, that is not the real reason. A blunt end will not pierce the threads of the canvas. The needles have numbers and are of different lengths. For the canvas sizes 10–14, I use either a #17 or #18 needle. You can buy them in packages of assorted numbers and sizes or of the same number and size, which I suggest you buy, since needles have a habit of disappearing—at least on me.

SCISSORS

There are scissors made just for needlepoint, but they always seem too small and delicate to me. So any size or shape will do. Only make sure they are sharp.

For the nearest store in your area selling supplies and materials, look in your telephone book under "Needlework" or "Arts and Crafts" retail.

The Stitches

I once read that there are over a hundred different stitches in needlepoint, and I believe it. Some seem to have several different names for the same stitch. For example, a bargello stitch could be called a flame or a Florentine. So as not to boggle the mind, I'm not showing you any novelty stitches. There is only one basic stitch in needlepoint and that is the tent stitch. However, there are three ways of producing this tent stitch and each one has a name. The first two I will only mention and will concentrate on the third, which is the basis for the designs in this book:

1. The half-cross stitch (done only on penelope canvas)
2. The basket weave stitch (done on mono canvas)
3. The continental stitch (done on mono canvas)

The only way to tell which method of stitch was used is to turn the canvas over and look at the back, since on the front surface all the stitches look the same. If they don't all slant diagonally from left to right and over one canvas mesh, a mistake has been made which can be corrected by what is called ripping (pulling out stitches, even if they are correct, to past the point of the mistake, using the end of the needle). It is not wise to use pulled-out yarn, since it has been weakened. Sew the weakened yarn under the last four or five good stitches on the back of the canvas, cut the yarn off, and start anew.

Now I have a confession to make. I knot the end of my strand of yarn to begin doing the continental stitch. In all the books I have read, this is frowned upon. I was taught this way and haven't had any bad results over the years for breaking this taboo. Knotting is a shortcut. Otherwise, you are supposed to start stitching, leaving one-half inch or more of yarn on the back and securing this yarn under your beginning five or six stitches each time you start a new strand. This is awkward and time-consuming for a beginner. The reasons given for not knotting are: (1) you might pull the knot out of the hole (well, make sure the knot is bigger and, if it does come through later on, poke it back down with the end of your needle); (2) the threads from the knots might be pulled through to the front of the canvas when working another color (just use your needle to pick the threads back through, or simply yank at the knot —the threads will come out); (3) you might be able to feel the knots when sitting on a finished chair cover or cushion. (This, I doubt!) I must say, however, that if you do knot, as I do, the backs of your canvases may be a bit messy looking, but just remember that only you and your professional finisher know what's on the back.

CONTINENTAL STITCH

Now that you have cut your first length of yarn (no more than 18 inches) and have pulled the third strand off, tie a knot at one end. Thread your needle and leave a couple of inches of yarn hanging loose from the eye. This end will tend to get longer and longer as you work the stitches. Just pull it up short again, but not too short or you'll constantly be threading your needle. Following the illustration of the continental stitch, bring the needle up at 1, making sure the knot stays there, down through 2 and pull it up through 3. Then go down through 4 and pull up through 5 and so on.

This will seem strange at first. It really is a push-and-pull method. Use both hands, push through with your right hand and pull through with your left hand. Switch the needle back to your right hand and push through and pull with the left. There is a constant switching of hands. (The other method I have seen used is similar to sewing—using only one hand for the pushing and then the pulling, which seems like a waste of both your hands and your time. It goes faster the other way.)

Eventually you will develop your own rhythm of working the stitching. When you come to the end of the design, cover the line with a stitch. Turn the canvas completely upside down and come back on the next row to the end of the design, again covering that line. Turn the canvas right side up and start the process all over again. And that is the continental stitch. One thing to remember—you have to turn your canvas upside down to come back on any second row of stitches.

As I mentioned earlier, the black lines in a coloring book correspond to outlining in needlepoint. In coloring books, however, you were told not to go over the lines, but in needlepoint, you do cover them. When you cover them in a different color than what the object is going to be, it is called outlining. This gives definition and delineates certain aspects of a design such as the veins on a leaf. There are certain ways of doing this in the continental stitch. The next three illustrations show you how: stitching vertically; stitching from left to right diagonally; and stitching from right to left diagonally. In all of these illustrations, you bring the needle up at 1, down at 2, up at 3, down at 4, and so forth, until you complete the line. When coming from right to left, you can form a straight line, but when you come from left to right you skip a hole. This will form a straight line only visually.

Now, when you have completed an area, or you have almost run out of the strands of yarn you are working with, you simply weave or sew into at least four or five stitches from the last stitch you put in, pulling slightly, and cut with your scissors. You are ready to start a new length of two strands where you left off or to start a new color. If the yarn left is too small to tie a knot with, throw it away. I save most yarn (but not that small) because you never know when you want just enough for two or three stitches.

There is another needlepoint stitch I have used, and that is for the background on the Peony Placemat design (see page 83). This is the Scotch stitch. All this is is a straight stitch going diagonally over five threads of the canvas to form a square. See the illustration: bring the needle up at 1, down at 2, up at 3, down at 4, and so forth, until you have completed the square. To start the next square, jump down to the next thread on the canvas and start doing the same steps as you have just finished. You do not cut the yarn to start the next square.

The other two stitches which I have used are

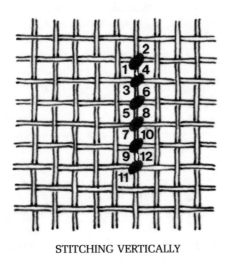

STITCHING VERTICALLY

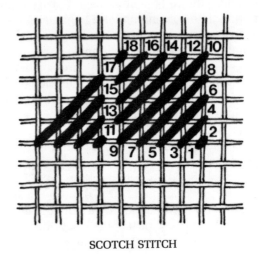

SCOTCH STITCH

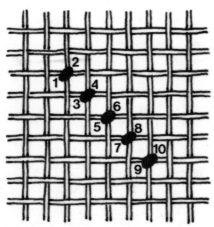

STITCHING FROM LEFT TO RIGHT DIAGONALLY

FRENCH KNOT

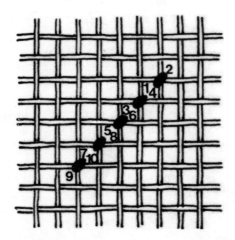

STITCHING FROM RIGHT TO LEFT DIAGONALLY

from the embroidery field of needlework and are put on after all the needlepoint stitches are worked. These are optional, but seem to add some zest to the finished work. Both use a single strand of yarn. The straight stitch is a single stitch laid out over the existing stitches to form a straight line, as in the whiskers on the Tiger Cats design (see page 104) or the leaf motif on the Peony Placemat (see page 83). Tie a knot, coming up from the back to form your line, going down through the stitches on top. The length of this straight line is up to you. There is really no correct way to tie this. If it looks good, keep it in. If it doesn't, pull it out and start over again.

The French knot is a tricky stitch. It looks simple, but trying to execute it is another matter. I started with this stitch in a kit that called for over one hundred French knots. I decided I had better learn to do this or the piece I was working on would never be finished. You are probably wondering what would call for all those knots. Well, it was to form foliage on trees. If I had picked a winter scene, I wouldn't have had to face this problem! But I'm glad I did. It is the added touch that looks so good. Follow the illustration: 1. Bring the needle up at (a), holding yarn with the other hand, twist the yarn once around the needle, go down at (b) and next to (a) as close as you can get. Pull out gently to complete the knot. Then sew under and cut the yarn. 2. The completed knot. The Pineapple Eyeglass Case design (see page 74) uses quite a few French knots.

Color

I just want to say a few words about the choice of colors for the designs in this book. I have picked colors that I like and feel are suited to the designs. This is all a matter of personal taste. I favor certain colors and shades. If you do not like my choices and have your own favorites, by all means use them. After all, you are doing the work, and you ought to like the colors, so have fun. That's what needlepoint is all about.

Getting It All Together

THE PATTERN

Just as in baking your own bread, cakes, and pies, you are going to start from scratch.

The first thing to do is to choose the design you want to make, then enlarge the pattern and color chart to the appropriate size, which is indicated at the beginning of each design. An easy way to do this is to take this book to a photostat house (look in your telephone book under "Photocopying"). Tell them you want the pattern blown up to the specified size. It's wise to do several patterns at a time since it is cheaper by the dozen. You will get back a negative and as many positive prints as you order. Save your negative print in case the positive print gets mutilated or lost. You can always order new prints from the negative. The cost of all this is nominal.

There is another way of enlarging designs called the grid method. This is done by transferring blocks or squares of the design to larger squares. You have to be able to draw reasonably well to do this, and it can be somewhat complicated according to the design, so I don't necessarily recommend it for beginners.

Tape your enlarged pattern to a big enough board or to a kitchen table, which makes a perfect working surface. Cut your canvas, leaving 2 inches or more around the design. This makes it easier for you to work with and easier for the finishing of the project, as I will explain later.

Buy an indelible marker, waterproof, that is. (There are many indelible markers made. A company named Nepo makes one just for needlepoint that comes in many different colors which can be helpful in highlighting certain difficult areas.)

Now tape your cut canvas over your pattern, centering it as well as possible. Trace the complete design onto the canvas. Anybody can trace, even if the lines are wobbly. Remember, all lines are covered. Sometimes the canvas threads will hide some of the pattern lines. Peel back the canvas to see where the lines are going, making sure you don't become off-centered.

At this point, some people like to paint in the various colors of the design and background. I find this a waste of time. You do have the color chart to follow. If you do decide to paint your canvas, buy waterproof acrylic paint. You are probably asking why I keep mentioning waterproof markers or paints. In the blocking process, in the finishing phases of your project, the canvas is sponged or even immersed in water. If you hadn't used waterproof markers or paints you can imagine what the canvas would look like—a complete disaster and nonsalvageable.

Before you begin stitching, bind your canvas edges with tape all the way around. This prevents you from catching your yarn on the stubs created when you cut the canvas. The stubs of the canvas can also fray your yarn, weakening it by the constant rubbing.

Where to start your stitches? This will be totally up to you. There are some basic rules about this though. The design is worked first. If there is any outlining within the design, this is done first. Background and borders are done last. Filling in a background can be boring, so you can divide your canvas up into four sections mentally, and work one section at a time for a change of pace. Just remember that the design is on your canvas, and there is no way you are going to lose it no matter how many mistakes you make. And you are going to make mistakes. I still do, mainly due to a lack of concentration. I once tried to watch a TV program while stitching. I skipped so many holes, I gave up and finished watching the program. Music seems to me to be the best background for needlepointing, preferably quiet and subdued, certainly not the "1812 Overture."

THE GRAPH

Looking at a graph can be frightening, especially if the color symbols are included on it, looking like one gigantic Chinese puzzle. That is why I have put the color guide on the pattern by num-

ber. Can you imagine coming up with twenty-six symbols for twenty-six colors? Sometimes you can't see the design for the symbols! Well, reading a graph is not that difficult. One square represents one stitch. That's all there is to it. *But* you have to count, count, and keep counting.

I have included a graph for each design for those people who know and love working with a graph and for the beginner, to show you just what I did in detailed areas that might otherwise seem confusing. You can go right to the graph and see how many stitches it took me and how that area of the design was made up.

To start a canvas using only the graph takes a great deal of time and a great deal of counting. Most books tell you to start stitching at the center of your canvas, which means you have to count the number of stitches in the horizontal border or background and divide by two to find that center. Then count the stitches in the vertical side of the border, divide by two, and that will be your center of your canvas. Hopefully, you haven't miscounted. I have worked only one canvas totally from a graph, and thank heavens it was only 5" × 7" and the design, which happened to be a zodiac sign, started three stitches in from the right-hand corner of the border. I worked down and across and it took forever, consulting the graph and counting.

What it all boils down to is this: use the pattern for your overall design, then consult the graph when you are baffled or bothered by certain areas that might not be too clear.

The Finishing Touches

Even though you have now put the final stitch in and breathed a sigh of relief, you are not quite finished. There are still two more rows of stitches to be done all around the border of the canvas of a square or rectangular design. On round designs, this is not necessary. The stitches can be of any color (you can use your leftover yarn). These added rows of stitching will be sewed or stapled under your finished pillow or wall hanging. If the design happens to have a border or solid background, try to remember to include the extra two rows of stitches while you are working. Then you will be all set.

After this chore is done, you are ready to hand your canvas over to a professional finisher. All

needlepoint has to be blocked to return it to its original shape. This involves blocking, stretching, and drying, an arduous and tiresome task. Just be glad someone else is doing it. Most shops have a professional finisher whom they use, or can certainly recommend someone. They also carry samples of material for backing of pillows and frames for wall hangings or pictures. Usually, the blocking is included in the price of the materials and workmanship. This part of needlepointing is the most expensive unless you have bought imported canvas and yarn. But it will be worth it when you see the final product. You have put in a lot of time on your canvas and you want it to look the best, so use a professional. Those of you who can sew and do framing will have no problem here. For the do-it-yourselfers, some basic instructions follow.

BLOCKING

Cover a board (plywood is excellent) that is larger than the canvas with brown wrapping paper. Tack the paper down using rustproof tacks. Measure and draw an outline of the correct dimensions of the stitched area of the canvas on the paper with your waterproof marker, making sure all corners are square.

Now soak your canvas completely in cold water. Wrap or roll it up in a bath towel to absorb some of the water. Never squeeze or wring it. Put the canvas facedown on the brown paper, aligning the design with the drawn dimensions. Tack it down at the bottom with 1/2-inch or 1-inch intervals. Pull or stretch and tack down the right side. Next, do the same at the top and finally the left side, always lining the canvas up on the drawn dimensions. Now allow this to dry completely (forty-eight hours) and *not* in direct sunlight. A staple gun can be used, but make sure the staples are rustproof. I find tacks are easier to pry up. Remove the canvas after drying and see if it is in the correct shape. If it isn't, you have to begin the whole process over again. You can see why I'm not fond of doing my own blocking!

PILLOW MOUNTING (KNIFE-EDGE)

Place your blocked canvas right side in (the design side), faced with the right side of the backing material you have chosen. Leave a seam allowance of two or more stitched rows all the way around. Pin or baste into place. Machine stitch or sew through all four corners, leaving most of the fourth side open. Trim any excess canvas and backing 5/8 inch from the stitching line. Then clip the corners for turning. Reverse the pillow casing, push out the corners, and stuff through the opening with pillow stuffing. By hand, sew up the opening with a whip stitch.

WALL-HANGING MOUNTING

Place your blocked canvas on a 1/8-inch Masonite board, allowing a 5/8-inch foldover of the two stitched rows. Now staple the canvas on the back, stretching it as you use the staple gun. Cut a piece of felt or backing material of your choice, and glue it over the stapled back. You can simply hang it as is or have it framed. There are now many frame shops that will cut the pieces and then you put it together yourself.

For more detailed information on blocking and mounting processes, go to your local library.

Part II
The Designs

Mr. Frog Toy

$14\frac{1}{4}'' \times 13\frac{3}{4}''$ **10 mesh canvas**   **#18 needle**

    This design was the very first piece of needlepoint I ever attempted. It was originally part of a bigger picture. There was a large daisy behind the frog. I eliminated that and enlarged the frog to make a stuffed toy for my niece.

    Since this is so simple a design with no outlining, it would be a good one to start learning the continental stitch with.

    Hint: I started with the black of the eyes and worked outward from there. You could also square the corners, add more background, and make a wall hanging for a child's room.

Mr. Frog Toy

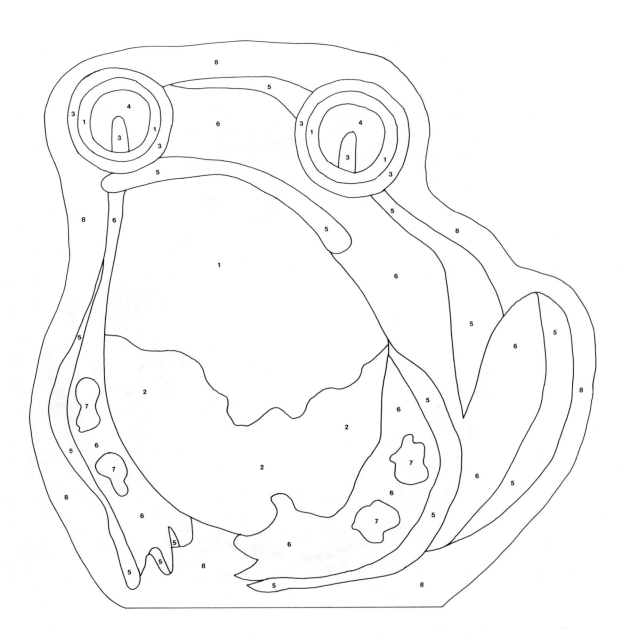

PATTERN AND COLOR CHART

1	White (12 yds.)		5	Forest green (8 yds.)
2	Pink (10 yds.)		6	Light olive (12 yds.)
3	Black (5 yds.)		7	Yellow (4 yds.)
4	Grass green (4 yds.)		8	Copper (10 yds.)

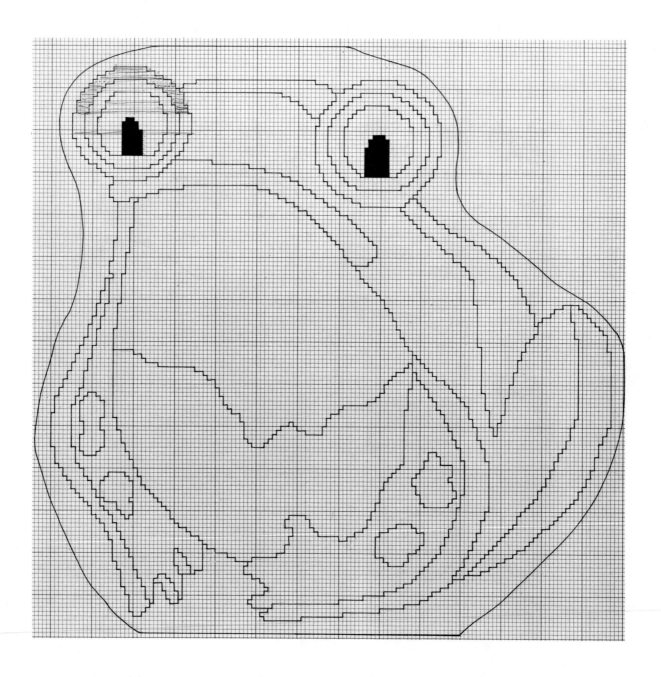

Fruit and Vegetable Pot Holders

7" × 7"   **10 mesh canvas**   **#18 needle**

Needlepoint pot holders may seem a little impractical, but they do look nice hanging on a kitchen wall. Another use could be as four hot-dish pads. If you worked all four designs as one unit, you would have an interesting and unusual placemat. Heat will not harm the wool, but you might want to cover the placemat with a sheet of Lucite or plastic to guard against messy eaters.

Hint: Start needlepointing at the top of each design and work downward, especially doing the veining on the apple leaf first.

Fruit and Vegetable Pot Holders

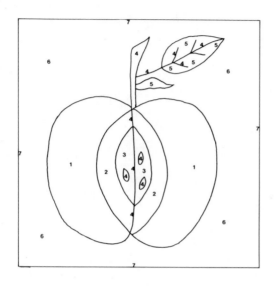

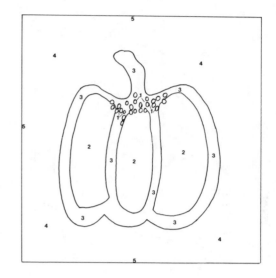

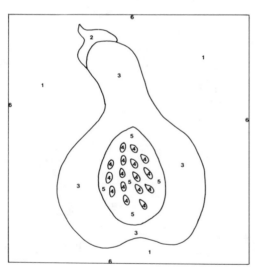

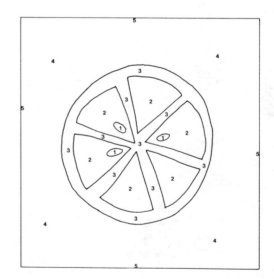

PATTERN AND COLOR CHART

APPLE

1 White (6 yds.)
2 Tan (3 yds.)
3 Yellow (2½ yds.)
4 Dark brown (2 yds.)
5 Grass green (1 yd.)
6 Cranberry (10 yds.)
7 Orange (1½ yds.)

PEPPER

1 Copper (½ yd.)
2 Lime green (5 yds.)
3 Bottle green (4 yds.)
4 Light olive (11 yds.)
5 Sky blue (1½ yds.)

SQUASH

1 Medium brown (10 yds.)
2 Lime green (1 yd.)
3 Light yellow (6 yds.)
4 Dark brown (1 yd.)
5 Tan (2 yds.)
6 Cranberry (1½ yds.)

LEMON

1 White (½ yd.)
2 Light mustard (3 yds.)
3 Dark gold (4 yds.)
4 Orange (10 yds.)
5 Olive (1½ yds.)

27

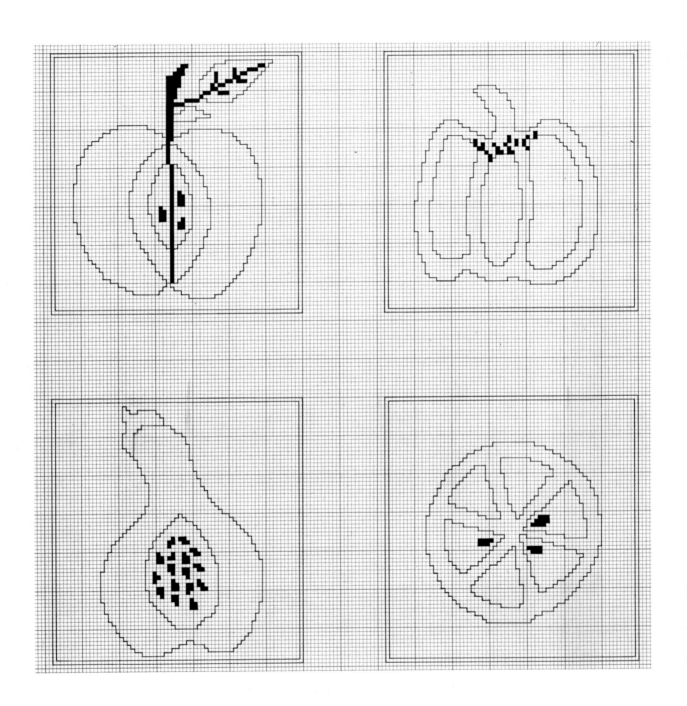

Lotus Quilt Pillow

14″ × 14″   **10 mesh canvas**   **#18 needle**

Quilting is more popular than ever. These next two designs are traditional and classic. There are hundreds of quilt patterns and they are easily adapted to needlepoint because they are so simple. If you have a favorite one, use it in place of my choice.

Hint: Fill in each square one at a time, starting in the upper right corner. Surrounding borders are done last. Here you can add your extra two rows immediately. These would make a lovely accent to any bedroom or den.

Lotus Quilt Pillow

PATTERN AND COLOR CHART

1	Red (12 yds.)	3	Grass green (16 yds.)
2	Orange (12 yds.)	4	White (36 yds.)

Lotus Quilt Pillow

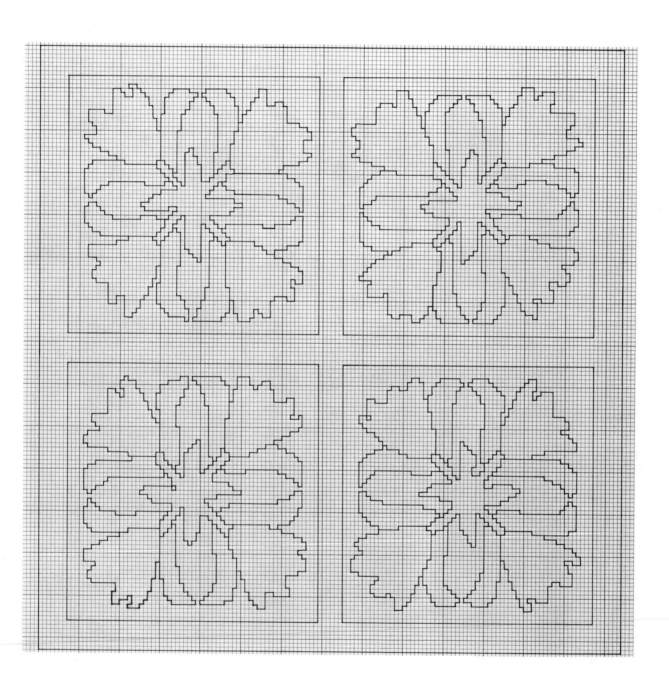

North Carolina Lily Quilt Pillow

14″ × 14″   10 mesh canvas   #18 needle

North Carolina Lily Quilt Pillow

PATTERN AND COLOR CHART

1	Orange (16 yds.)	4	Deep purple (14 yds.)
2	Green (12 yds.)	5	White (36 yds.)
3	Magenta (6 yds.)		

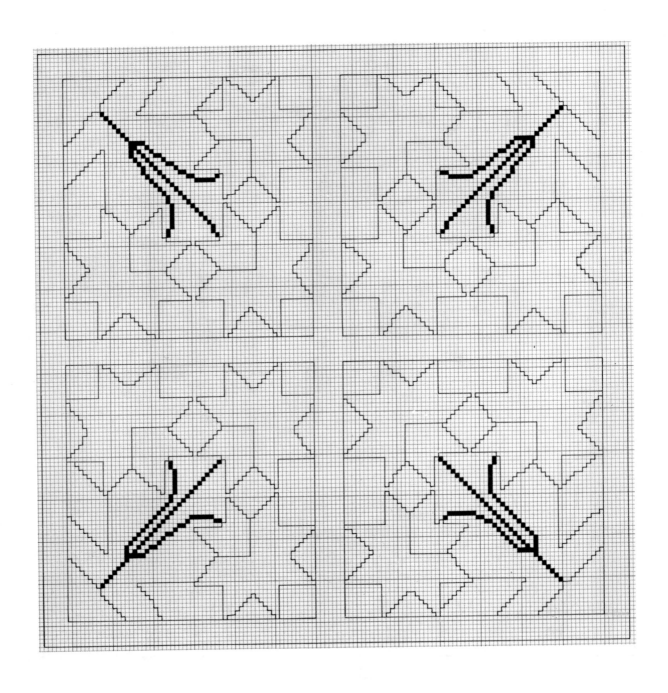

Wild Strawberries Pillow

10″ × 12¹/₂″   **12 mesh canvas**   **#18 needle**

June is my favorite month because it's strawberry-picking time. And if you can find them, wild strawberries are the best. I can't seem to get enough of them.

Hint: Do the cranberry sections of the strawberries first, then fill in with red. Next, the centers of the flowers, then the petals. The greenery is last for the design. The pattern in the border has to be done first before filling in. Start in the upper right-hand corner, coming down diagonally, jumping from each "x" without tying off until you come to the end of the row. The centers of the flowers contain French knots; see the pattern or graph for placement.

I gave this pillow to a friend who put it on a white wicker couch with white canvas cushions on a sunny porch. It looked terrific. Of course, you couldn't have missed it.

PATTERN AND COLOR CHART

1	Lime green (16 yds.)		7	White (6 yds.)
2	Olive (6 yds.)		8	Yellow (2 yds.)
3	Forest green (8 yds.)		9	Dark gold (1/2 yd.)
4	Dark green (3 yds.)		10	Bright green (14 yds.)
5	Cranberry (2 yds.)		11	Royal blue (6 yds.)
6	Red (8 yds.)			

Peruvian Parrot Pillow

14″ × 15³/₄″   10 mesh canvas   #18 needle

In 1967, I took a trip to South America. In Lima, Peru, in the museum, I found this design incised on a jar. I made a sketch. The jar was from the Florescent Period (A.D. 400–800), unearthed at Nazca, below Lima. The lightning bolt border is a typical Inca motif.

Hint: I began with the eye, then the head and worked downward. The border, of course, is last.

I have this pillow in my den surrounded by many pieces of pottery and objects collected from South America. My sister liked it so much I made one for her living room.

Peruvian Parrot Pillow

PATTERN AND COLOR CHART

1	Black (8 yds.)		4	White (10 yds.)
2	Brown (10 yds.)		5	Yellow (7 yds.)
3	Royal blue (14 yds.)		6	Red (60 yds.)

Beach Rose Chair Cushion

13¹/₂″ diameter   10 mesh canvas   #18 needle

These next four designs were made out of necessity. My mother could not find replacements for a set of cushions that had become old and frayed at her beach cottage. I told her I would make some for her. And since I like to visit the summer place, it was a nice gift.

Hint: All flowers should be done first, starting with the centers. The foliage last. These could also be made into four separate knife-edge pillows or one gigantic one for practically any room in the house.

PATTERN AND COLOR CHART

1	Pink (60 yds.)	5	Bottle green (10 yds.)
2	Cranberry (5 yds.)	6	Olive (7 yds.)
3	Rose (4 yds.)	7	Grass green (1 yd.)
4	Dark pink (4 yds.)	8	Lime (1 yd.)

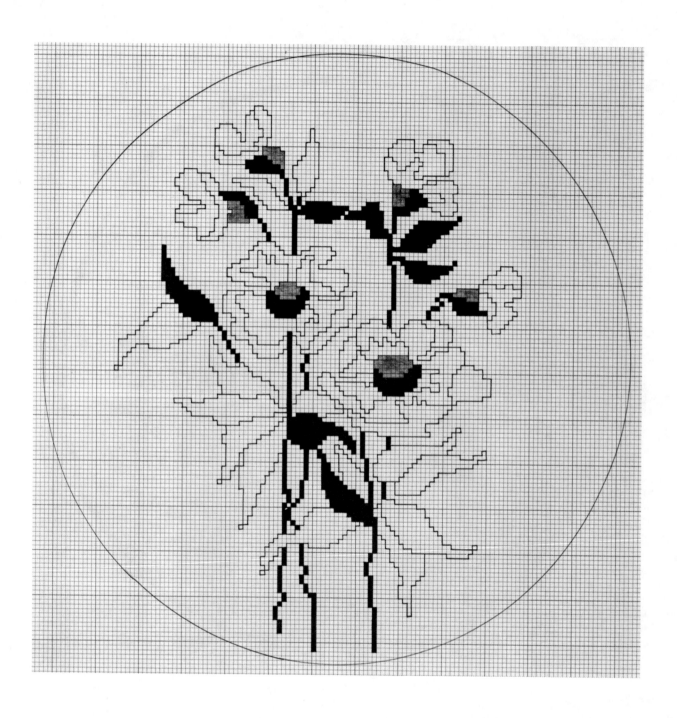

Summer Violets Chair Cushion

13¹/₂″ diameter   **10 mesh canvas**   **#18 needle**

PATTERN AND COLOR CHART

1	Robin's egg blue (70 yds.)		6	Pale lavender (6 yds.)
2	Yellow (5 yds.)		7	Dark green (3 yds.)
3	Deep orange (4 yds.)		8	Forest green (4 yds.)
4	Purple (4 yds.)		9	Deep olive (6 yds.)
5	Lavender (5 yds.)			

Summer Violets Chair Cushion

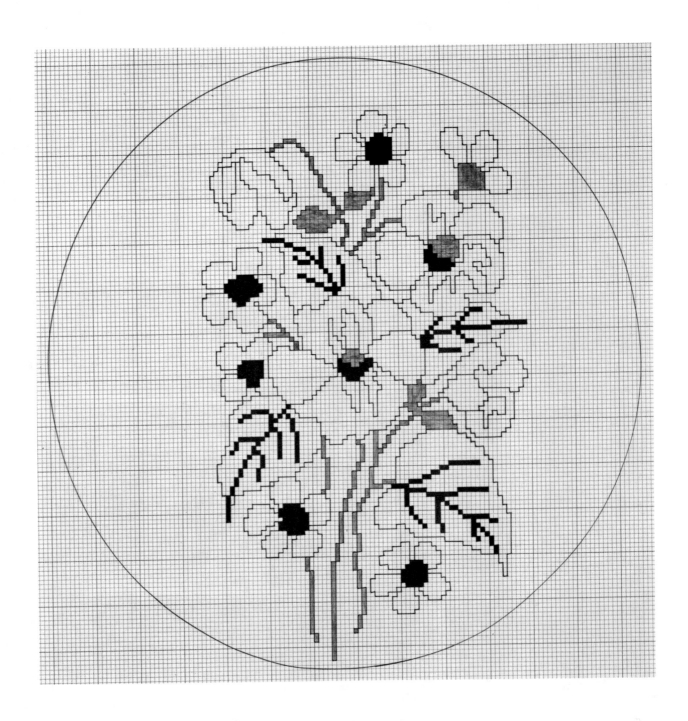

Wild Asters Chair Cushion

13$\frac{1}{2}$″ diameter   10 mesh canvas   #18 needle

PATTERN AND COLOR CHART

1	Light mustard (70 yds.)	7	Gold (4 yds.)
2	Dark orange (4 yds.)	8	Dark gold (3½ yds.)
3	Orange (3 yds.)	9	Grass green (6 yds.)
4	Light orange (1 yd.)	10	Pale green (5 yds.)
5	Tan (1 yd.)	11	Lime green (1 yd.)
6	Dark brown (½ yd.)		

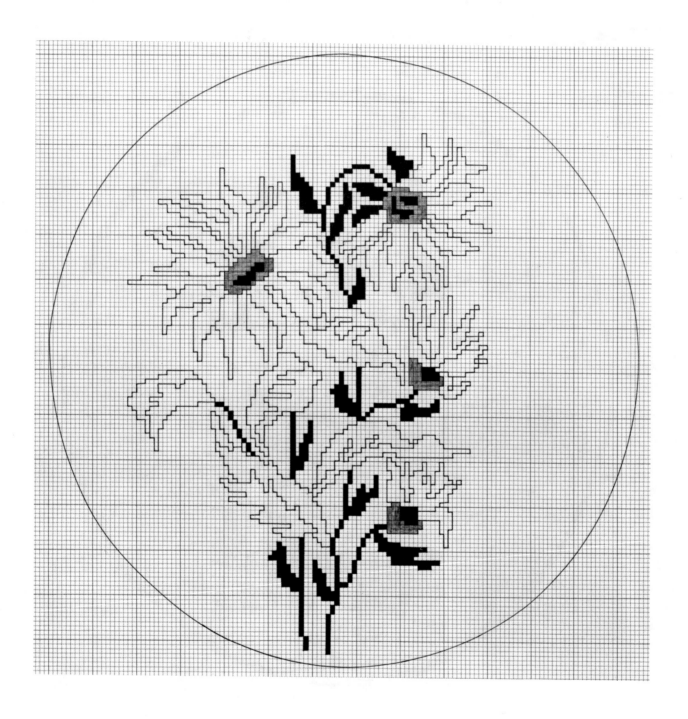

Spring Bouquet Chair Cushion

13½″ diameter   10 mesh canvas   #18 needle

PATTERN AND COLOR CHART

1	White (70 yds.)		5	Dark green (7 yds.)
2	Yellow (6 yds.)		6	Bottle green (7 yds.)
3	Dark orange (3 yds.)		7	Royal blue (7 yds.)
4	Red (2 yds.)			

Spring Bouquet Chair Cushion

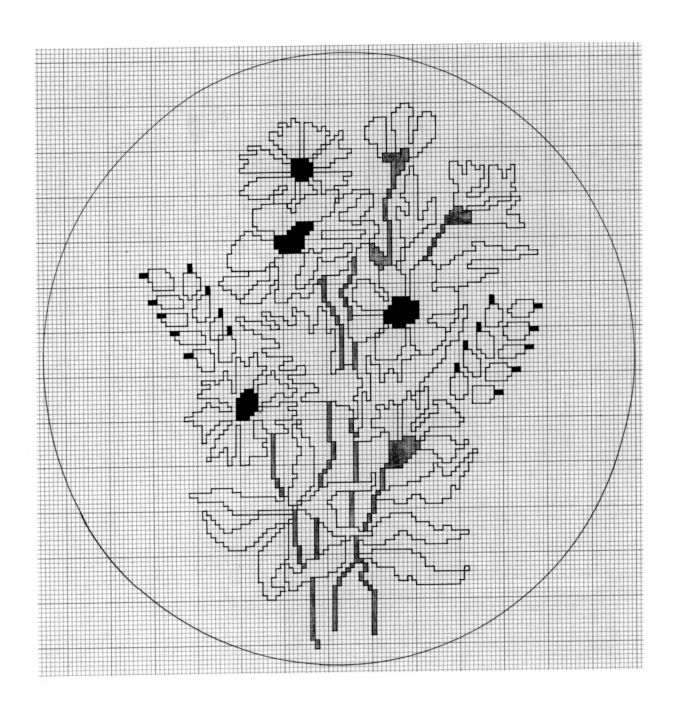

Baseball Stamp Pillow

11″ × 15″   10 mesh canvas   #18 needle

As a boy growing up, I played baseball, but, unfortunately, I was not very good at it. I also collected stamps, which I was better at, as long as my piggy bank held out. When this stamp was issued, I bought one and saved it. Years later I decided it would be fun to do in needlepoint.

Hint: Start stitching with the red hat and work down. I always like to start at the top of a design and work down. This is just a quirk with me. You can start at any point you choose. This pillow is suited to a boy's room or, framed, it would go nicely in a game room.

Baseball Stamp Pillow

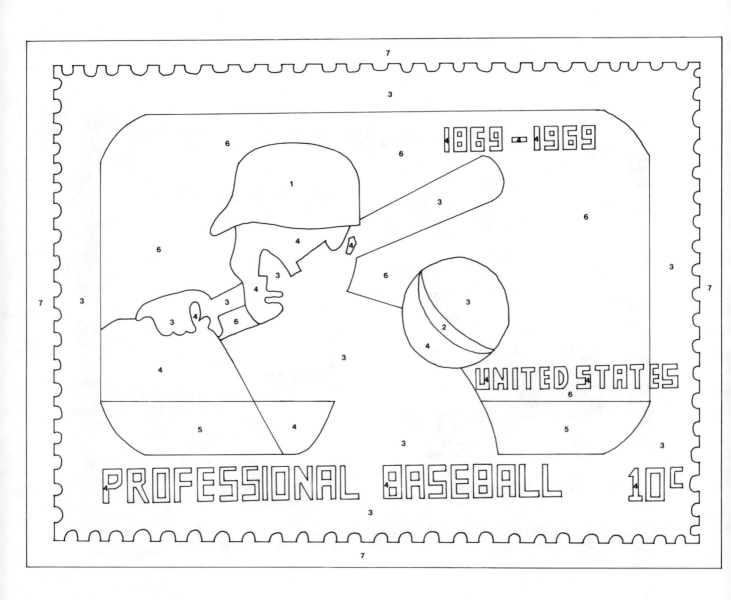

PATTERN AND COLOR CHART

1	Red (4 yds.)		5	Grass green (5 yds.)
2	Dark gray (2 yds.)		6	Light mustard (14 yds.)
3	Off-white (24 yds.)		7	Brown (10 yds.)
4	Black (6 yds.)			

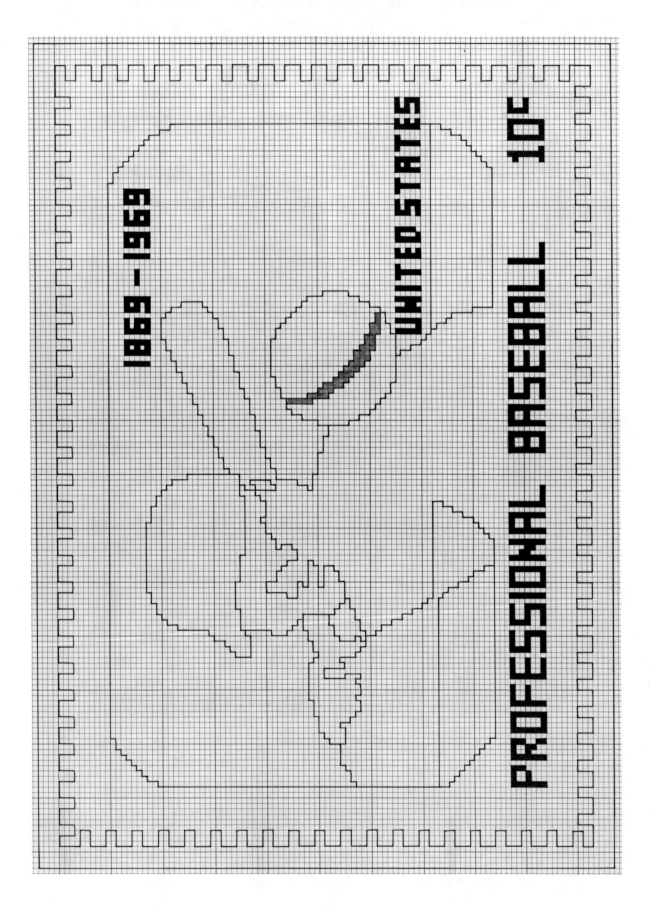

Tomatoes and Leeks Picture

8″ × 10″   12 mesh canvas   #18 needle

In the late sixties, I was a designer for a dish towel company and did a lot of drawings of vegetables and fruit. It was great fun and the drawings adapt to needlepoint so easily.

Hint: The tomato on the right should be done first since it overlaps the other tomato. Then you can work outward in any direction. The outlining of the green leaves of the leek has to be done first before filling them in. This picture adds a touch of color to my kitchen wall. It would also make a nice cover for an album for your favorite recipes.

56

Tomatoes and Leeks Picture

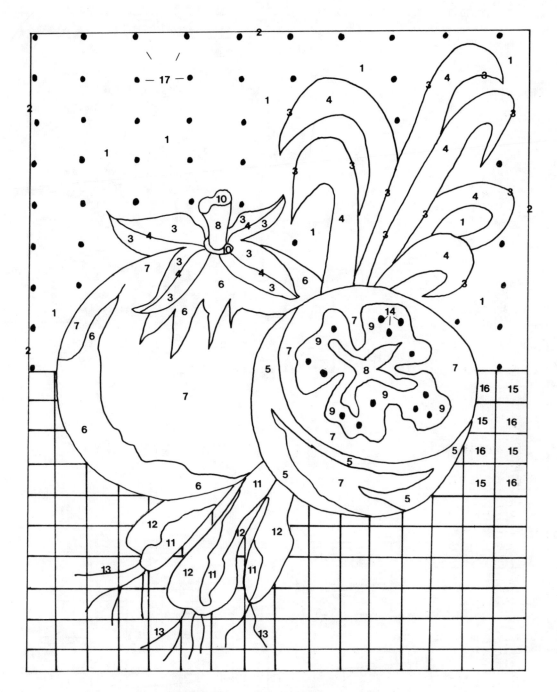

PATTERN AND COLOR CHART

1	Sky blue (12 yds.)		10	Ochre (1/2 yd.)
2	Orange (2 yds.)		11	Tan (2 yds.)
3	Dark green (4 yds.)		12	Khaki (2 yds.)
4	Grass green (4 yds.)		13	Silver gray (1 yd.)
5	Cranberry (3 yds.)		14	Dark brown (1/2 yd.)
6	Maroon (3 yds.)		15	Black (10 yds.)
7	Red (6 yds.)		16	White (10 yds.)
8	Light olive (1 yd.)		17	Lavender (3 yds.)
9	Pink (2 yds.)			

Spring Chickens Picture

14″ × 14″   10 mesh canvas   #18 needle

I came across this design on a ceramic tile that I bought at a flea market. A friend of mine bought a chicken farm some time after that, so for a gift I adapted the design for a needlepoint picture. He has it hanging in his office. If you don't have a chicken farm, you can hang it in your kitchen.

Hint: Do the outline of the chickens' combs, wattles, and beaks first, then work down, doing any outlining first before filling in. This would also make a fun pillow.

Spring Chickens Picture

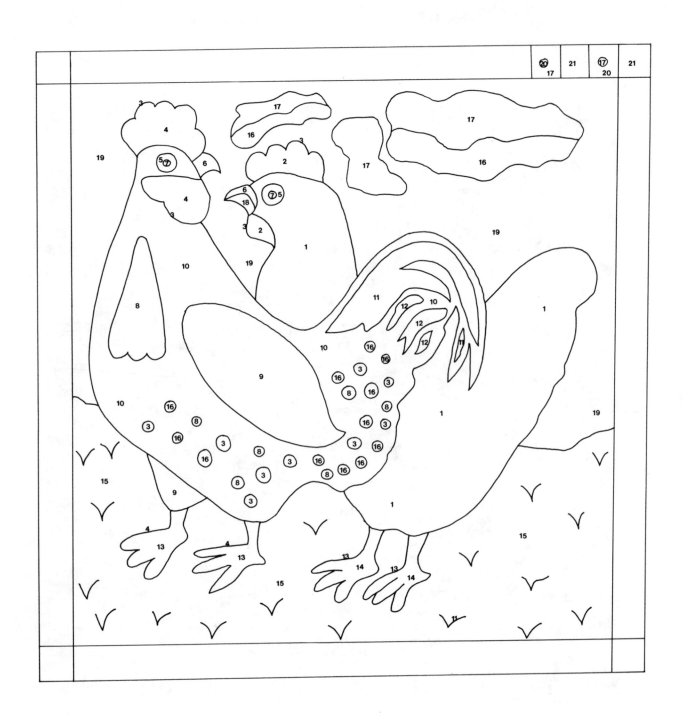

PATTERN AND COLOR CHART

1	Dark gray (10 yds.)	8	Tan (2 yds.)	15	Light olive (14 yds.)		
2	Geranium red (1 yd.)	9	Sienna (3 yds.)	16	Cream (1 yd.)		
3	Cranberry (1/2 yd.)	10	Cocoa (10 yds.)	17	White (12 yds.)		
4	Red (3 yds.)	11	Dark green (4 yds.)	18	Ochre (3 yds.)		
5	Yellow (1/2 yd.)	12	Grass green (11/2 yds.)	19	Sky blue (15 yds.)		
6	Gold (1/2 yd.)	13	Dark orange (1 yd.)	20	Bright gold (12 yds.)		
7	Black (1/2 yd.)	14	Orange (1 yd.)	21	Prussian blue (12 yds.)		

Spring Chickens Picture

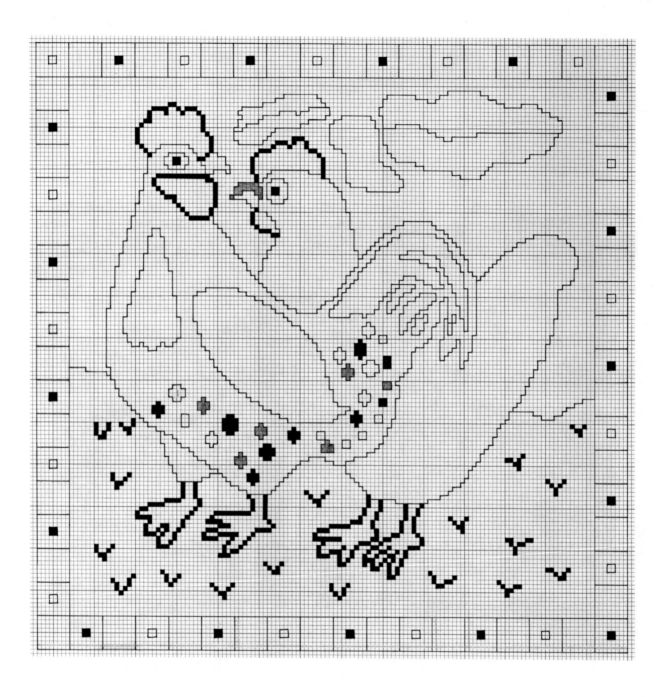

Seashell Pillow

11″ × 15¼″   10 mesh canvas   #18 needle

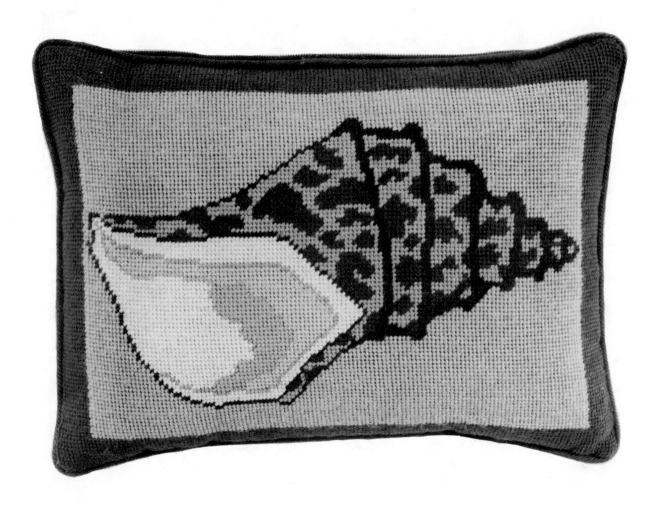

    I collect everything from stamps to beach glass, and seashells too. Nature provides such interesting and fascinating patterns. The shape of the shell is like a New England Neptune whelk with the spotted look of a Junonia volute. This was my second canvas design.

    Hint: All outlining is done first—including the silhouette of the shell and the lip.

    I originally wanted this to be an insert under a glass-top table, but couldn't find one small enough. I think it's still a nice idea.

Seashell Pillow

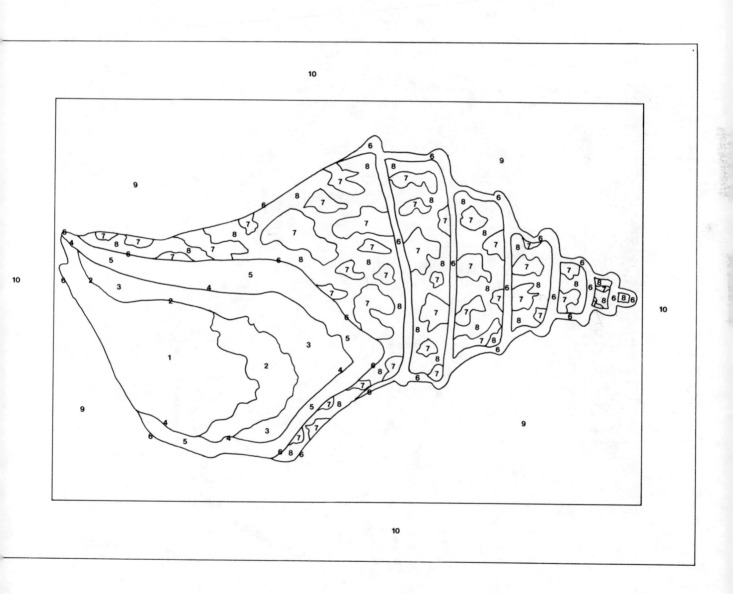

PATTERN AND COLOR CHART

1	Pink (4 yds.)		6	Dark brown (5 yds.)
2	Rose (3 yds.)		7	Rust (7 yds.)
3	Dusty rose (3 yds.)		8	Cocoa (10 yds.)
4	Khaki (1 yd.)		9	Sand (24 yds.)
5	Off-white (2 yds.)		10	Cranberry (18 yds.)

Seashell Pillow

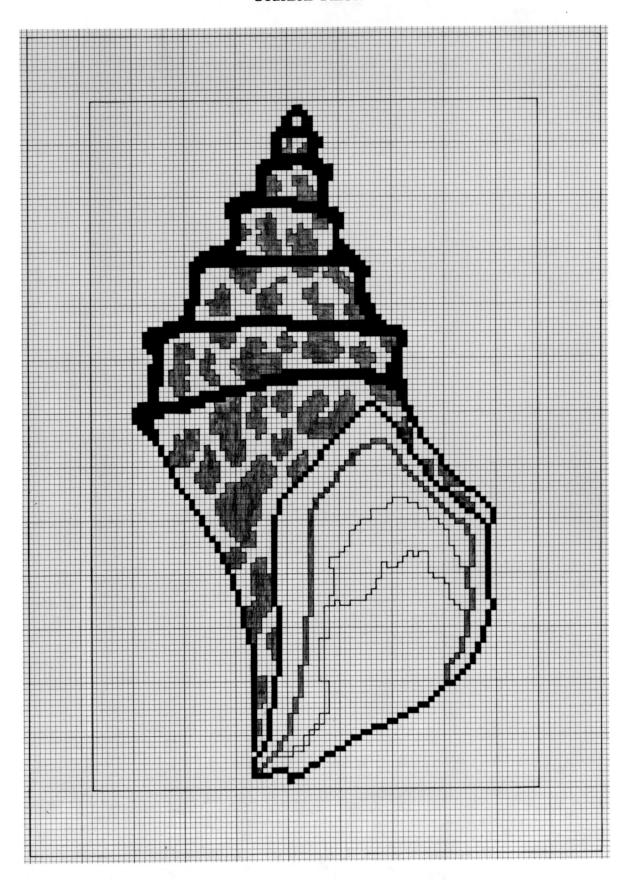

PINEAPPLE EYEGLASS CASE AND SEA HORSE EYEGLASS CASE

FRUIT AND VEGETABLE POT HOLDERS

JACK OF SPADES PILLOW

DUCK DECOYS PICTURE

TIGER CATS PILLOW

GUATEMALAN DOVES PILLOW

TOMATOES AND LEEK PICTURE

CHICKEN TEA COZY

Holly Wreath

13½″ diameter   12 mesh canvas   #18 needle

I've always hated parting with my Christmas wreaths. Each year I'd save the pine cones and fake berries and buy a plain wreath to decorate the next year. Then I thought, why not make a permanent wreath in needlepoint? So, voilà.

Hint: The pine cone outlining comes first since it overlaps the holly leaves, berries next, and finally the leaves.

You can fill in the hole if you wish and make a round pillow for any season.

Holly Wreath

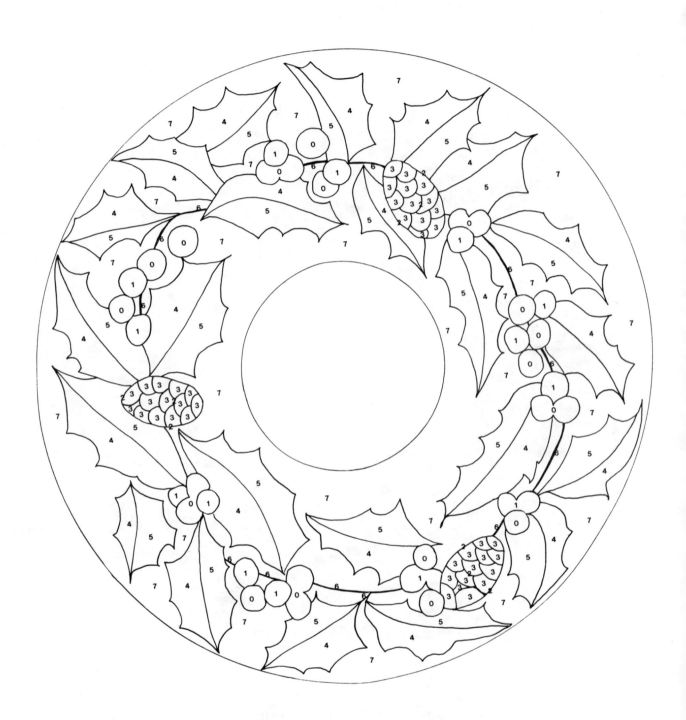

PATTERN AND COLOR CHART

0	Cranberry (6 yds.)		4	Olive (16 yds.)
1	Geranium red (5 yds.)		5	Dark green (16 yds.)
2	Dark brown (2 yds.)		6	Forest green (3 yds.)
3	Brown (4 yds.)		7	White (24 yds.)

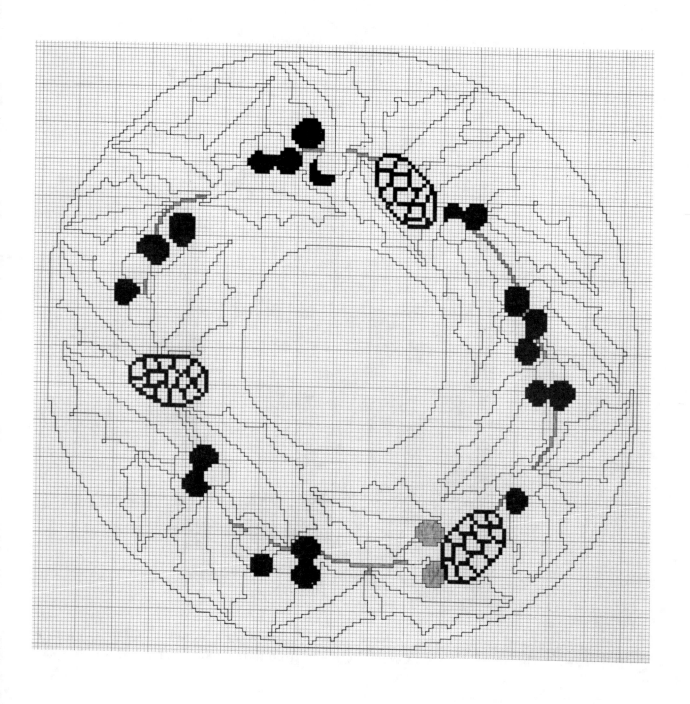

New England Town Picture

9″ × 16″   12 mesh canvas   #18 needle

This design and the following covered bridge design were adapted from the lath art of the Dutch artist, Theodore DeGroot. Originally made from narrow strips of wood, the pieces were fitted together like a jigsaw puzzle.

Here you will get a workout in outlining in every direction, since practically everything in the designs is outlined.

Hint: Start at the upper right-hand corner with the outlining and come down. You can do these designs in sections, doing the outlining first and then filling in. This way you will not get bored with the outlining.

A nice pair of pictures for your den or library.

New England Town Picture

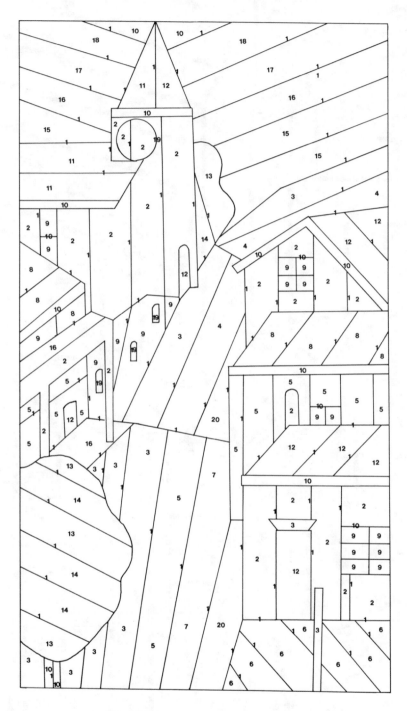

PATTERN AND COLOR CHART

1	Black (16 yds.)	8	Dusty rose (5 yds.)	15	Beige (3 yds.)
2	White (14 yds.)	9	Gray (4 yds.)	16	Gold (6 yds.)
3	Rust (8 yds.)	10	Cream (4 yds.)	17	Mustard (6 yds.)
4	Copper (4 yds.)	11	Royal blue (4 yds.)	18	Pale yellow (4 yds.)
5	Light brown (7 yds.)	12	Prussian blue (6 yds.)	19	Magenta (1 yd.)
6	Dark brown (4 yds.)	13	Moss green (4 yds.)	20	Cocoa (3 yds.)
7	Tan (3 yds.)	14	Dark green (4 yds.)		

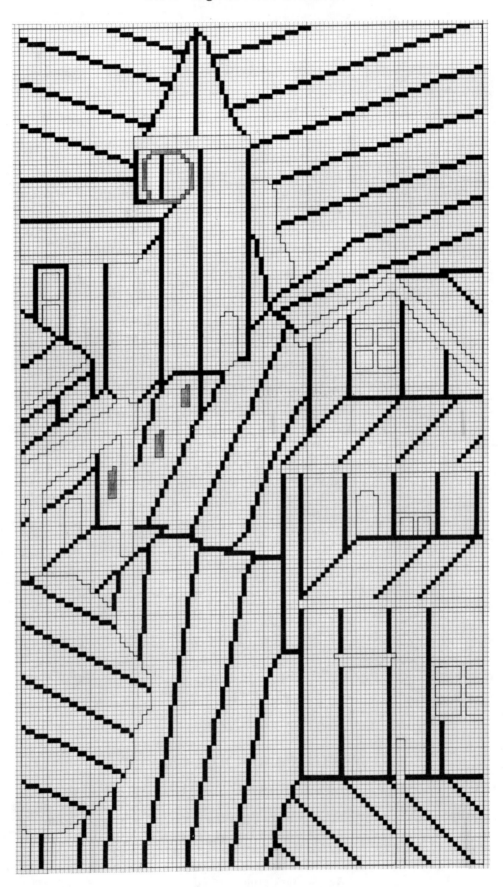

Covered Bridge Picture

12" × 15"   12 mesh canvas   #18 needle

Covered Bridge Picture

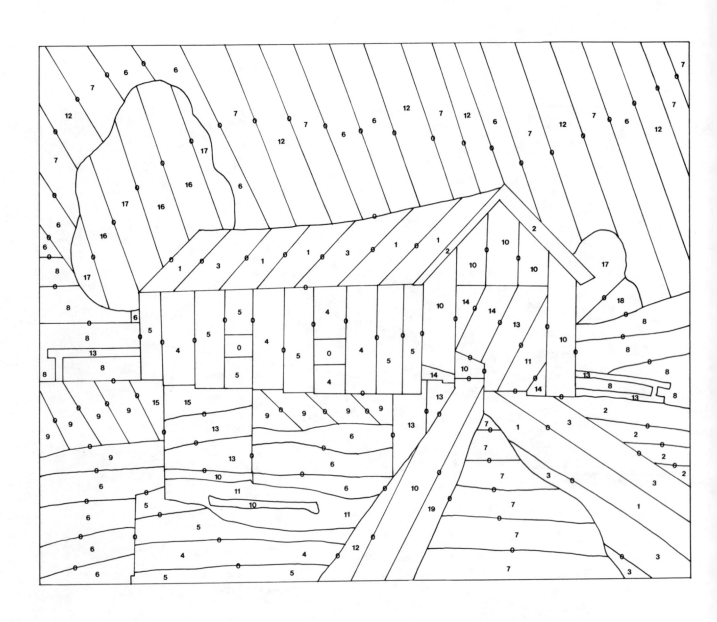

PATTERN AND COLOR CHART

0	Black (18 yds.)	**7**	Sand (16 yds.)	**14**	Steel blue (6 yds.)
1	Brown (6 yds.)	**8**	Tan (6 yds.)	**15**	Cobalt blue (2 yds.)
2	Dark brown (3 yds.)	**9**	Light olive (6 yds.)	**16**	Moss green (5 yds.)
3	Copper (4 yds.)	**10**	White (5 yds.)	**17**	Olive (5 yds.)
4	Red (6 yds.)	**11**	Navy (3 yds.)	**18**	Dark green (1½ yds.)
5	Dark red (6 yds.)	**12**	Natural (12 yds.)	**19**	Cocoa (2 yds.)
6	Cream (12 yds.)	**13**	Gray (4 yds.)		

Covered Bridge Picture

Pineapple Eyeglass Case

7¼" × 7"   14 mesh canvas   #18 needle

I read somewhere that the pineapple is a sign of hospitality. Probably, it is in Hawaii. Whatever the origin, the finished case makes a perfect gift for spectacle wearers.

Hint: The outlining in the pineapple leaves is done first; fill in with green. Then come the sections of the pineapples. After completing all the needlepoint, put in the French knots indicated on the pattern and graph by black dots.

You can blow up the pineapple design to a much larger size to make a banner with the word WELCOME.

Pineapple Eyeglass Case

PATTERN AND COLOR CHART

1	Brown	(20 yds.)	4	Copper	(14 yds.)
2	Green	(8 yds.)	5	Dark brown	(2 yds.)
3	White	(10 yds.)			

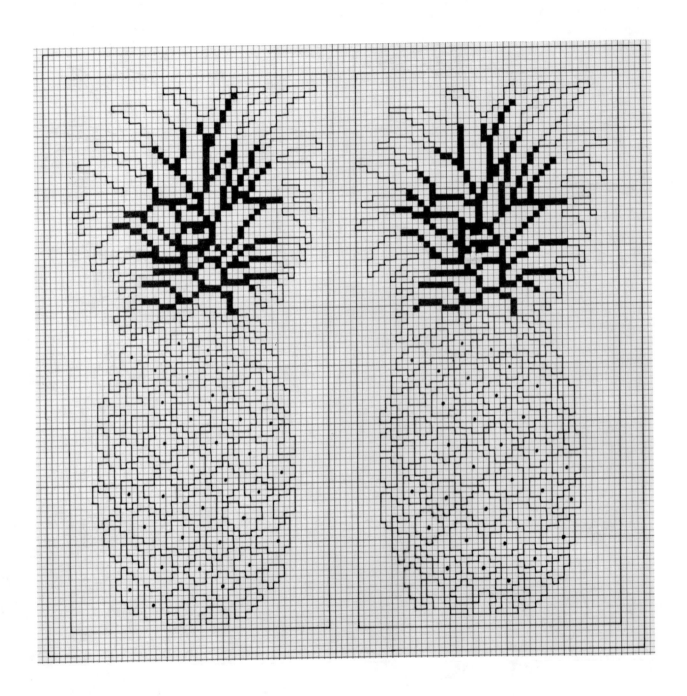

Sea Horse Eyeglass Case

7¹/₄″ × 7″   12 mesh canvas   #18 needle

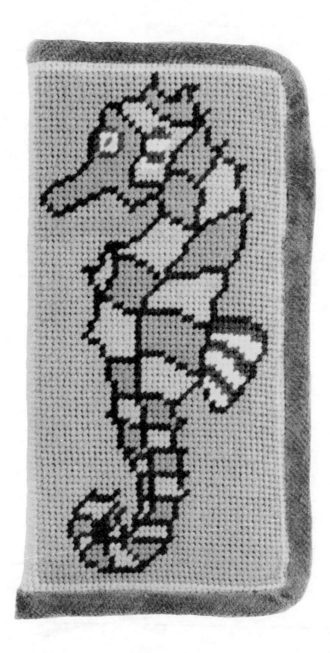

The first time I ever saw a live sea horse was in an aquarium in Buffalo, New York, at an early age. They have intrigued me ever since. I bumped into one a few years ago while scuba diving in the waters off St. Thomas, Virgin Islands. I made this eyeglass case for my hostess while vacationing in the Caribbean.

Hint: The sea horses have to be completely outlined before putting in the other colors. Start at the top and work down.

Using the sea horse design in various sizes, you could create an interesting pillow.

Sea Horse Eyeglass Case

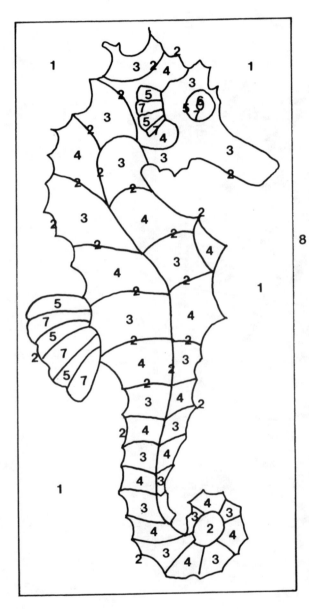
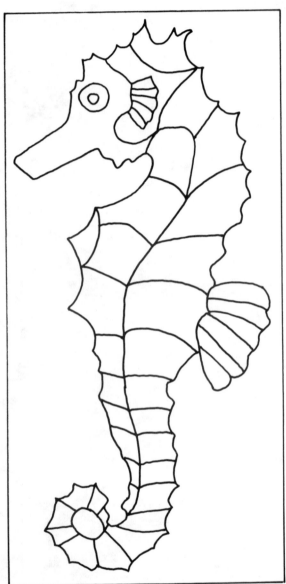

PATTERN AND COLOR CHART

1	Light olive (20 yds.)		5	Royal blue (4 yds.)
2	Navy (8 yds.)		6	Emerald green (1/2 yd.)
3	Turquoise (10 yds.)		7	White (2 yds.)
4	Robin's egg blue (10 yds.)		8	Light aqua (10 yds.)

Sea Horse Eyeglass Case

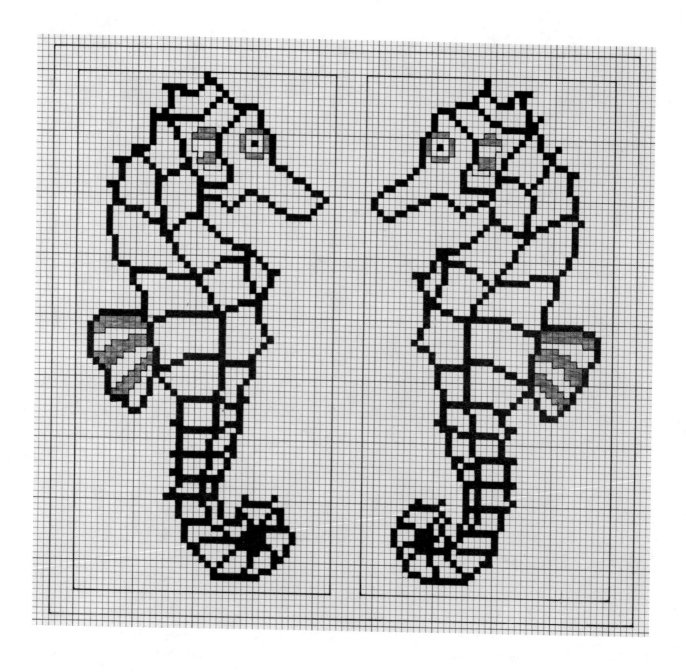

Leopard Heraldic Pillow

15" × 15"   **12 mesh canvas**   **#18 needle**

After my junior year in college, I spent the summer traveling through Europe. In Florence, Italy, I bought two scarves with this heraldic design on them. Several years later, I had them made into a pillow cover. The material gradually wore thin and started to fade. So I made a pattern and adapted it to needlepoint. Now I have a pleasant reminder of that year and my stay in Italy.

Hint: The leopard outlining and leopard spots are done first. Fill in the rest of the body. The eye of the leopard is a French knot in black and the whiskers are one strand of black in the straight stitch put on after all needlepoint is completed.

Leopard Heraldic Pillow

PATTERN AND COLOR CHART

1	Powder blue (36 yds.)		5	Red (72 yds.)
2	White (18 yds.)		6	Black (1/2 yd.)
3	Gold (14 yds.)		7	Ochre (2 yds.)
4	Dark brown (9 yds.)			

Leopard Heraldic Pillow

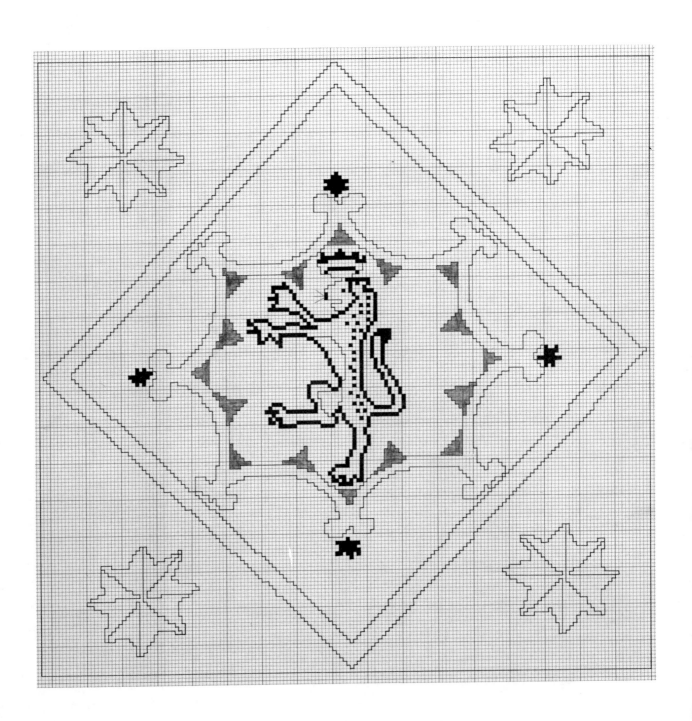

Peony Placemat

18″ × 12″   12 mesh canvas   #18 needle

On first thought, this may seem impractical, but not if you cover the needlepoint with Lucite cut to fit over the placemat for protection.

Hint: Outline the big peony first and fill in with the other colors. Work outward to form the circles of the plate. The straight stitches of leaf pattern on the napkin are put on last over the needlepoint. For placement, see the pattern.

The background of the mat is done in the Scotch stitch illustrated on page 16. The starting point for this stitch is indicated on the graph.

If you have a favorite pattern on your own dinnerware, make a tracing and substitute it for this one.

Peony Placemat

PATTERN AND COLOR CHART

0	Rusty brown (18 yds.)	5	Dark green (4 yds.)	10	Dark lavender (10 yds.)
1	Medium gray (12 yds.)	6	Bottle green (6 yds.)	11	Orange (1 yd.)
2	Silver gray (10 yds.)	7	Fern green (6 yds.)	12	Magenta (1/2 yd.)
3	Peach (8 yds.)	8	Rose pink (6 yds.)		
4	Coral (4 yds.)	9	Pale lavender (72 yds.)		

Peony Placemat

Chicken Tea Cozy

12″ × 11¼″   12 mesh canvas   #18 needle

Everybody likes a good hot cup of tea now and then. No better way to keep the pot warm but with a tea cozy. The English are so practical. This makes a wonderful gift for any weekend host or hostess.

Hint: Begin with the hen's comb and work downward, doing any outlining, then filling in with the other color. The background design is done next. Here you will have to count down to place each X pattern. There are nine stitches separating each X coming downward. It seems to go faster if you do one stripe at a time. The brown speck on the beak is a French knot.

This can also double as a toaster cover when not in use as a cozy. Or you could square off the top and turn it into a small pillow or picture.

Chicken Tea Cozy

PATTERN AND COLOR CHART

0	Black (4 yds.)		**5**	White (2 yds.)		**10**	Sky blue (12 yds.)
1	Dark brown (10 yds.)		**6**	Copper (1 yd.)		**11**	Geranium red (1/2 yd.)
2	Gold (7 yds.)		**7**	Cranberry (2 yds.)		**12**	Dark orange (3 yds.)
3	Brown (14 yds.)		**8**	Pink (12 yds.)		**13**	Olive (4 yds.)
4	Yellow (1/2 yd.)		**9**	Red (2 yds.)			

Chicken Tea Cozy

King of Diamonds / Queen of Hearts
Wall Hanging

14³/₄" × 15¹/₂"   **10 mesh canvas**   **#18 needle**

For one of my art projects in college, I chose to do an illustrated history of the playing card which had to include an original design. This is my design, adapted for needlepoint.

Hint: I started with the king's crown and worked downward. The outlining of the face and features has to be done before filling in with the flesh color. The completed canvas was then backed with felt and has a knobbed metal rod through it at the top for a banner effect which is not shown in the picture. It would make an interesting pillow, too, for any game room.

PATTERN AND COLOR CHART

0	Dark brown (4 yds.)	6	Dark gray (4 yds.)	12	Magenta (4 yds.)
1	Black (7 yds.)	7	Flesh (6 yds.)	13	Prussian blue (8 yds.)
2	Gold (6 yds.)	8	Purple (8 yds.)	14	Light olive (6 yds.)
3	Mustard (2 yds.)	9	Red (6 yds.)	15	Pale yellow (70 yds.)
4	Silver gray (5 yds.)	10	Copper (3 yds.)	a	White (1/2 yd.)
5	Medium gray (4 yds.)	11	Geranium red (2 yds.)		

King of Diamonds/Queen of Hearts Wall Hanging

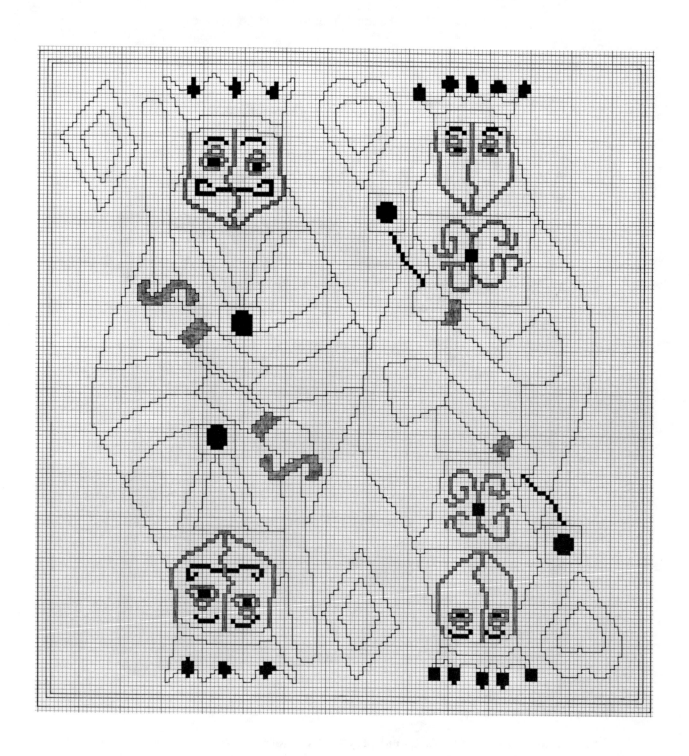

Jack of Spades Pillow

11¹/₂″ × 14″   **12 mesh canvas**   **#18 needle**

This design is taken from an actual playing card found in Provence, France, dating around 1440. It was the first known printed playing card made from a wood block. The French called the figure a knave or valet.

Hint: There is quite a bit of outlining in this pattern, so start at the top with the hat and work down, filling in as you go.

I had this made into a boxed pillow to give the effect of a playing card. It is the perfect accent for a den or game room.

Jack of Spades Pillow

PATTERN AND COLOR CHART

1	Cobalt blue (4 yds.)	6	Copper (2 yds.)	11	Natural (48 yds.)
2	Olive (5 yds.)	7	Black (12 yds.)	12	Gold (2 yds.)
3	Forest green (7 yds.)	8	Rust (4 yds.)	13	Flesh (2½ yds.)
4	Red (9 yds.)	9	Brown (3 yds.)		
5	Light rust (10 yds.)	10	Steel gray (3 yds.)		

Stitch three rows of black all the way around to form border.

93

Duck Decoys Picture

11½″ × 15½″   12 mesh canvas   #18 needle

My mother collects decoys of any size, shape, and material, so I decided to design this needlepoint piece for her birthday and her collection.

Hint: Start with the lower duck's head since it overlaps the other duck. Remember, outlining has to be done first. A mat around the needlepoint was added and gives it a little more zest. A pillow would be nice, too, or even an album cover.

Duck Decoys Picture

PATTERN AND COLOR CHART

1	Black (15 yds.)	7	Silver gray (9 yds.)	13	Medium brown (4 yds.)
2	White (7 yds.)	8	Steel gray (5 yds.)	14	Light olive (8 yds.)
3	Bright gold (3 yds.)	9	Gray (6 yds.)	15	Bottle green (7 yds.)
4	Rust (10 yds.)	10	Brown (3 yds.)	16	Dark green (5 yds.)
5	Copper (7¹/₂ yds.)	11	Jade green (4 yds.)	17	Cranberry (2 yds.)
6	Emerald green (5 yds.)	12	Fawn brown (6 yds.)	18	Navy (48 yds.)

Duck Decoys Picture

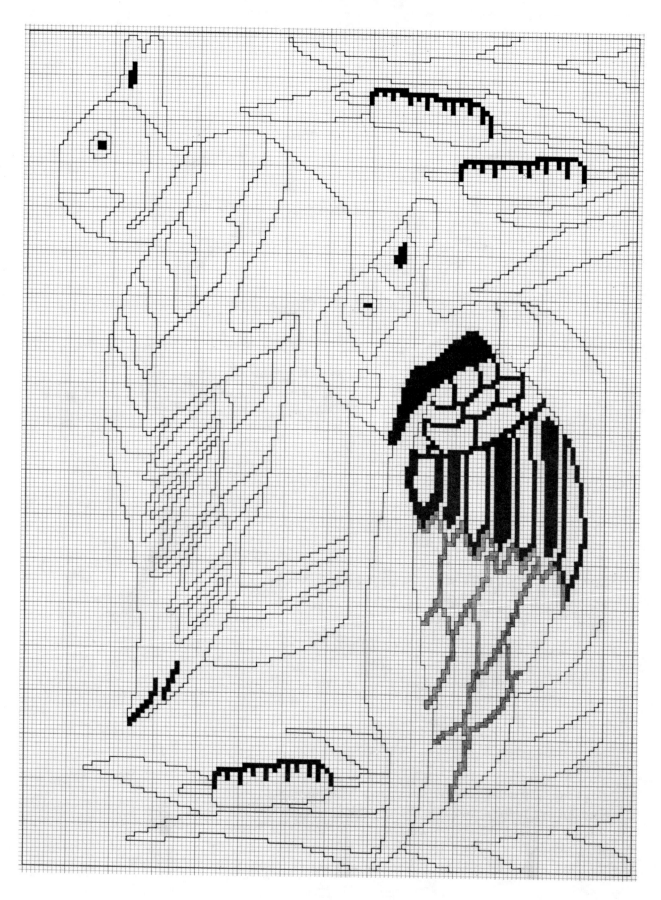

Mr. Pig Picture

14″ × 14″   12 mesh canvas   #18 needle

When you have a big family, you never run out of projects to complete. Around birthdays and Christmas, everyone knows what to expect from me! This project was designed for my niece's daughter, Nicole. She called it Mr. Pig.

Hint: The complete pig is outlined, as well as the features and bow ribbon. These have to be done first. I actually started at the tail. French knots of one strand of white complete the eyes. Instead of a picture, how about a pillow for a child's bed?

Mr. Pig Picture

PATTERN AND COLOR CHART

1	Baby blue (13 yds.)	7	Medium gray (5 yds.)	13	Yellow (3 yds.)
2	Pink (4 yds.)	8	Prussian blue (4 yds.)	14	Deep orange (3 yds.)
3	Natural (5 yds.)	9	White (14 yds.)	15	Orange (3 yds.)
4	Dark gray (9 yds.)	10	Rose (1 yd.)	16	Grass green (15 yds.)
5	Black (7 yds.)	11	Dark green (6 yds.)	17	Navy (1½ yds.)
6	Battleship gray (7 yds.)	12	Forest green (1 yd.)	18	Turquoise (3 yds.)

Shorebird Picture

14″ × 16″   **12 mesh canvas**   **#18 needle**

    While growing up, I spent every summer at the seashore and became familiar with the family of birds that abounds there, from sea gulls and terns to the little sandpiper. This design is of a sand plover.

    Hint: The bird should be completed first until it meets the grass. The dark grass blades are done next, followed by the bottle green and olive colors, then the silver gray silhouettes.

    This would make a striking pillow, also.

Shorebird Picture

PATTERN AND COLOR CHART

0	Silver gray (12 yds.)		7	Copper (6 yds.)
1	Dark green (9 yds.)		8	Gold (3 yds.)
2	Olive (10 yds.)		9	Dark brown (4 yds.)
3	Bottle green (9 yds.)		10	Ochre (3 yds.)
4	Black (12 yds.)		11	Tan (3 1/2 yds.)
5	White (13 yds.)		12	Sand (60 yds.)
6	Rust (4 yds.)			

Six rows of black to form the border.

Shorebird Picture

Tiger Cats Pillow

13½″ diameter   12 mesh canvas   #18 needle

I have three cats, and my first book, *The Needlepoint Cat,* was inspired by my affection for felines. This is a new design, created for fellow cat lovers.

Hint: Begin with the large cat's ears and work down and across. The bows and rug are outlined. For placement of the cat's whiskers, check the pattern and color chart.

This was made into a boxed pillow. Round pillows should be boxed. Otherwise, they tend to look flat. A boxed pillow or cushion gives a trim, tailored look to your finished needlepoint. This is accomplished by using strips of fabric, usually the same as the backing and with welting. The length of the strips is the perimeter or circumference of the pillow or cushion plus a ½-inch seam allowance at each end. Its width is optional and depends on how plump you want your pillows.

104

Tiger Cats Pillow

PATTERN AND COLOR CHART

1	Moss green (11 yds.)	9	Dusty rose (1/2 yd.)	16	Tan (1/2 yd.)
2	Black (8 yds.)	10	Gold (7 yds.)	17	Dark orange (1 yd.)
3	Dark gray (4 yds.)	11	Pink (1 yd.)	18	Light olive (2 yds.)
4	Gray (4 yds.)	12	Brown (5 yds.)	19	Dark olive (4 yds.)
5	Silver gray (9 yds.)	13	Dark brown (2 yds.)	20	Bottle green (7 yds.)
6	Cream (3 yds.)	14	Copper (6 yds.)	21	Teal blue (14 yds.)
7	Cranberry (1 yd.)	15	Sand (4 yds.)	22	Light blue (1/2 yd.)
8	Royal blue (2 yds.)				

One strand of white for whiskers using the straight stitch over the existing needlepoint.

Goldfish Aquarium Picture

14″ × 15¹/₂″   **12 mesh canvas**   **#18 needle**

Everyone must have owned a goldfish at some time in his or her life. I can remember going to the dime store and buying a little glass bowl and one fish, carrying it home in a Chinese paper carton. The fish didn't last very long, and I made many trips back to the dime store for replacements. Years later I splurged and bought a large tank and exotic fish, everything from bubble-eyes to Japanese carp. And that is where the inspiration for this design came from.

Hint: The fish and grass are all outlined. Do the fish, one at a time, first, then the grass. I started with the bubble-eyed goldfish at the upper top of the picture. I like to start at the top and work down.

Goldfish Aquarium Picture

PATTERN AND COLOR CHART

0	Royal blue	(48 yds.)
1	Lime	(10 yds.)
2	Bottle green	(14 yds.)
3	Light olive	(14 yds.)
4	Olive	(6 yds.)
5	Dark green	(6 yds.)
6	Dark orange	(9 yds.)
7	Orange	(6 yds.)
8	Pumpkin	(4 yds.)
9	Black	(6 yds.)
10	White	(14 yds.)
11	Light mustard	(5 yds.)
12	Cranberry	(2 yds.)
13	Red	(4 yds.)
14	Silver gray	(6 yds.)
15	Gold	(3 yds.)
16	Dark gold	(1 yd.)

Goldfish Aquarium Picture

Guatemalan Doves Pillow

14″ × 14″   12 mesh canvas   #18 needle

This design comes from one of the many bark paintings of Mexico and Guatemala. Usually, they were painted in neon-glow colors. I bought one that happened to be unpainted and adapted it to needlepoint using more subdued shades.

Hint: The dove outlining in black comes first. The flowers next, working out from the centers, followed by the foliage. Bottom border and background last. This design would also be stunning framed in dark wood for your living room wall.

PATTERN AND COLOR CHART

1	Royal blue (60 yds.)		7	Bottle green (10 yds.)	
2	Gold (8 yds.)		8	Dark green (5 yds.)	
3	White (24 yds.)		9	Black (14 yds.)	
4	Rose (6 yds.)		10	Copper (3 yds.)	
5	Pink (6 yds.)		11	Light tan (6 yds.)	
6	Light olive (8 yds.)